I Was Thinking
Conversation Starters to Use with Loved Ones with Cognitive Loss

By Diana Waugh, RN, BSN

———————■———————

Dedication

I dedicate this workbook to the millions of elderly Americans who suffer from cognitive loss, and to their families who want to continue showing them love and devotion.

Acknowledgments

I would like to thank:
- My Mom, Iona Kiser, who taught me invaluable lessons every day of my life.
- My mentor, Sister Michael Sibille, who taught me to look at the psychosocial aspects of the aging.
- My colleague, Becky Dorner, who wouldn't let me give up on writing.
- My friends who tried this approach, found it helpful, and encouraged me to write it in order to share it with others.
- My editor, Jennifer Bays, who took my writing and made it work.
- Most importantly, my husband, Gary, our children, Kent, Kevin, and their families, who always believed in me, and provided the push to complete this project!

———————■———————

Rewarding Conversations in the Face of Cognitive Loss

I WAS THINKING is a workbook that helps people better communicate with their loved ones suffering with cognitive loss. It is a guide that can lead to happy, calm conversations. The information discussed in this book may be new and different from what you have heard before. However, it truly has the potential of reconnecting you with a loved one you may have felt was lost to you because of cognitive loss.

———————— ■ ————————

I'VE BEEN THERE

I am writing from my experience as a daughter of a mom who suffered from cognitive loss. I am writing as a nurse who has worked with residents in long-term care facilities for more than 30 years. I am writing because I believe I have a couple of tips that can help you enjoy your loved ones even when cognitive loss has changed them from the people you once knew.

I am not writing as an expert. I am not writing as a researcher with lots of data and statistics to share. I will share some techniques that work sometimes, but not every time. I am writing because I feel if you can increase your positive interactions with your loved one by just 25 percent, my experience will not have been in vain.

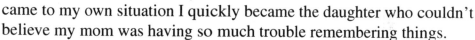

As a child of a mom with cognitive loss, I have made all of the mistakes! Oh sure, I teach the "correct way," but when it came to my own situation I quickly became the daughter who couldn't believe my mom was having so much trouble remembering things.

I know how it felt when I tried to help her as she began to have difficulty with short-term memory. I would call to talk about her day—what she had done, what she ate, and who she had visited. Of course, she couldn't remember and both of us would get frustrated with our conversation. I would finish the uncomfortable conversation, feel bad it had not gone well, and then beat myself up for not being more understanding.

Time would pass, and the next time we would get together I would make the same mistakes! Not because I'm not bright, but because I couldn't accept that the Mom I knew was leaving me. The person who remained was very nice, but different from my mother.

It is from this experience that I want to offer you some thoughts and approaches to conversing with your loved ones. I also want to share some of the rationale as to why these approaches may work for you.

Throughout this book, the phrase *cognitive loss* will be used to identify the condition where a person has short-term memory loss and problems making decisions. It is not indicative of any specific diagnosis, such as Alzheimer's disease or any specific type of dementia. This workbook will help you focus on what to say, what not to bring up, and most importantly, what to talk about.

CAN YOU GIVE THEM UP?

Sometimes it seems that if you "give up" on your loved ones as you knew them, you can "find them" in a different way. Growing up, we expected that our parents would always be all-knowing, all-wise, and always available to us. After all, they have been telling us they are right since we were children!

Probably one of the most difficult, but most helpful approaches to having good conversations is to let go of our expectations of them. We need to stop looking at them as we always have. We need to change our expectations so we aren't constantly frustrated and saddened by their lost abilities. When we change our expectations, we can find them as they are. We can have meaningful conversations. Our approach will not add to their confusion and anxiety. Our relationship, although different, will be so much more fulfilling. It will provide us with happy memories of the latter part of their lives.

"Give Them Up" Examples

Sounds easy; let's see how this works in real life situations. Let's take a look at several conversations and find the reason for the success or lack of success in each one.

Example One:

> Son: Dad, would you recommend buying that stock you told me about yesterday or not?
>
> Dad: I don't know what you are talking about.
>
> Son: Of course you do. You were telling me what was best just yesterday.
>
> Dad: (Frustrated) Well, whatever I told you is right. Why do you keep asking? Do what I told you. Leave me alone!

And, we're off and running!

Let's try it again with the same people, but a different conversation.

> Son: Dad, I was just thinking about how proud you were when you told me to buy the SYZPQR stock. It really did well for me. Thanks a lot.
>
> Dad: Anything I can do for you, you just let me know.

In the first example, the son was holding on to previous expectations of his dad and his dad's abilities. The question was too demanding. The father didn't want to look inadequate. When the son pushed, the dad got frustrated and fired back. The conversation was not successful for either person.

In the second conversation, the son was able to give up his expectations of his dad. He still took his knowledge of his dad's successes and turned the conversation into a success for both of them. Notice the dad's response; he felt he was still being helpful, and even offered future help.

10

Example Two:

Daughter: Hey, Mom. Yesterday you said you were going to bake your famous chocolate chip cookies. Why didn't you do it?

Mom: I wasn't hungry for them.

Daughter: You always told me that it's important never to say you are going to do something and then not do it. Now you are doing just that.

Mom: (Crying) Now you're upset with me. I want to make you happy. I can't do anything right anymore.

Same topic with a little different perspective...

Daughter: Hi, Mom. I was wondering if you had a chance to make your famous chocolate chip cookies recently?

Mom: No, I wasn't hungry for them.

Daughter: I was wondering if you would share your secret for perfect cookies?

Mom: Well, if you promise to keep it a secret...I always use butter.

Daughter: OK, thanks for sharing your secret. I'll give it a try.

Mom: Let me know if it works. Do you need my recipe?

Daughter: I think I already have it. I'll let you know if I can't find it.

Again, we see that the difference in the outcomes of the conversation is the expectation of ability. In the first conversation, the daughter was trying to remind her mom of a task her mom had not completed. It came across like a reprimand because of the reference to her mom's lack of compliance with a belief her mom once held. In the second conversation, the daughter used the chocolate chip cookie topic, but didn't challenge her mom to defend her lack of action. This exchange allowed the mom to maintain the feeling that she is helping with a topic she enjoys discussing.

FORBIDDEN WORDS

If we were to make a list of things to avoid when talking with our loved ones, that list would be headed by the word "No," and the phrase, "Do you remember?" Our loved ones see these words as a test. The words offer a challenge, and more devastatingly, a reminder that what they are saying or doing is wrong.

There are other words we might not use in conversation, but we may think them. These include, "He's being manipulative," "She knows better," "He's being deceptive," and "She's lying." We think that our loved ones can control or change their thinking. However, due to their cognitive loss we might very well be asking more than they can do. If we have these thoughts when conversing with them, it sets us up to be at odds with our loved ones. No one wins.

THE DREADED WORD, "NO"

If we can remove one word from our vocabulary when talking with loved ones, it should be, "No."

Let's think back to when we were children. Adults told you, "No, don't do that," "No. You can't do that," or "No, that's not correct." Can you remember how you felt when you heard any of those sentences? The adults were trying to help you. They were trying to protect you from harm, or keep you from making a mistake. But most importantly, these types of statements kept you from doing what you wanted to do.

Were you pleased with the adults' concern for you? Unless I miss my guess, you weren't happy being told "no."

We are no different just because we're older. Hearing that dreaded word at any age has a similar effect.

I learned how true this is from my son and daughter-in-law as they began raising their children. If you have observed young parents, you will find a very sparing use of the word "No." The reason they give for not using the word as often is because of the negative connotation and the devaluing of the child's thoughts.

Even if the idea of never saying "no" again makes sense to you as a concept, how do you make it work in real life?

Even though our loved ones are losing their short-term memory, there is still good news. If they remain calm and content, their ability to carry a thought begins to reduce. That sounds contrary to reason, doesn't it? Let's see if this makes sense to you.

Have you ever been having a happy, calm conversation with someone and find yourself saying, "Now, what was I talking about?" This is what occurs for our loved ones on an ever-increasing frequency.

The rule of thumb is that without confrontation, people with cognitive loss will lose their train of thought in about five minutes. Of course, people are all different, so that time might vary. If they remain calm, their forgetfulness will often take the topic away from them.

The good news is this basic human trait can be helpful when memory loss is present. Have you ever had a difference of opinion with someone and have absolutely no problem remembering your position? This also occurs for your loved one. Even when they no longer can make logical decisions, they know and feel their position, and their concern is real. Their actions usually tell us that they feel their position is either being ignored or is being dismissed when they state an idea and hear "No."

By refraining from telling our loved ones they are wrong, that their decision isn't good, or what they want to do is unacceptable, they will stay happier and calmer. It will also increase the likelihood that they will forget their point within a few minutes and confrontation can be avoided.

The most challenging yet most rewarding approach to talking with loved ones with cognitive loss is to learn to live in *their* reality, not yours.

"No" EXAMPLES

All right, but how do you manage this when you are in a real life situation?

Let's look at several conversations and find the reason for the success or lack of success in each.

Example One:

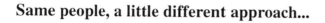

Dad: I've got to go back to my barn.

Daughter: No, Dad, you don't have your barn anymore.

Dad: Yes I do! I need to go there right now!

Daughter: No. You sold it several years ago.

Dad: No, I would never sell it! Take me there now!

Same people, a little different approach...

Dad: I've got to go back to my barn.

Daughter: That was a great barn. I really liked the white windows. Was it hard to paint them? They were so high!

Dad: Well, you had to be strong. I used that big ladder. Remember?

Daughter: Yes, I do. It was the one you always told me to stay off of!

Dad: I loved that barn. It's gone now.

Or,

Dad: I've got to go back to my barn.

Daughter: What do you need to do there, Dad?

Dad: I've got to check on the horses and their food.

Daughter: Do you think we might need to get some horse food for them? What should we check?

Dad: Check their hay and oats. We might need straw for their stalls too.

Daughter: Let me get a piece a paper. You think we need hay...oats....straw for bedding. Anything else?

As you can see, the stories you know about your loved one become very important as you are driving the conversation to a calm, comfortable outcome. These are the kinds of stories you will want to record on the pages provided at the back of this workbook.

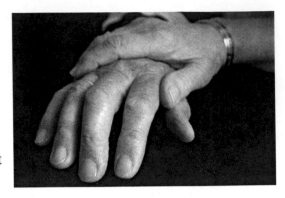

Example Two:

Brother: I've got to get going and get to work.

Sister: No. You don't work anymore; you are retired!

Brother: That's not true. They are waiting for me, and can't start the day without my direction.

Sister: You are wrong.

Brother: I'm not wrong. You are trying to keep me a prisoner here.

And, we're off and running!

Same people, a little different approach...

Brother: I've got to get going and get to work.

Sister: You were so important at the airplane engine plant. I was thinking about the time you took me on a tour of the building. Wow, those engines were huge! How much did they weigh?

Brother: Well, it depended on the model. Some were heavier than the others. Do you remember the time I took you for a ride in that biplane?

Redirecting the conversation based on topics stored in long-term memory can assist you in moving the discussion from one that can very easily anger your loved one, to an enjoyable conversation of sharing old memories.

THE CONFRONTATIONAL "DON'T YOU REMEMBER?"

While asking "Don't you remember?" is intended to help prompt our loved ones, it is often heard as a quiz.

Think back to an occasion where someone asked you if you remembered a particular person or situation. You really couldn't recall the time, yet the person kept saying, "Of course you remember. They used to live on Elm Street. They had that black dog. They always stopped to talk. You remember, right?"

At each prompt, you state that you really can't remember. However, the person keeps adding more and more pressure until you suddenly say, "Oh! Right. Sure, I remember that." Of course, you then hope there are no more follow-up questions!

This is what I believe occurs in the minds and hearts of people with cognitive loss. "Saving face" is simply a part of life. It is not comfortable to be wrong or be on the outside looking in. The more you question them, the more they try to stay in the conversation.

However, the memory loss leads to frustration; the more frustration that occurs, the greater the chance that a confrontation will occur. When confrontation happens, everyone feels loss.

"DON'T YOU REMEMBER?"

All right, but how do you manage this when you are in a real life situation?

Let's look at more conversation snippets and try to find the reasons why the conversations succeeded or not.

Example One:

Mom: Someone just told me my mother is dead! That's not true.

Son: Sure it is, Mom. Don't you remember? She died years ago.

Mom: No she didn't! She's waiting for me to visit her!

Same people, but a little different conversation...

Mom: Someone just told me my mother is dead! That's not true.

Son: Tell me the neatest thing about your Mom.

Mom: She made wonderful cherry pies!

Son: I love cherry pies.

Mom: My mother liked me better than my brothers, so she would save a piece of pie for me when I got home from school.

Son: Talking about that is making me think of food. I'm going to get a cup of coffee. I'll bring you one too.

Mom: See if you can find some cherry pie!

Or,

Mom: Someone just told me my mother is dead! That's not true.

Son: Your mother was a wonderful grandma to me. I was thinking about her cherry pies. She used to set them on the windowsill to cool. I was always thinking the birds would eat them!

Mom: She watched the birds very closely. She would never let them close enough to eat those great pies. I loved them so.

Again, the best way to have a positive outcome to your conversations is to take the history you have and make it work for both of you.

Example Two:

Husband: Who are those strangers in the pictures on my dresser? Why are they there?

Wife: Don't you remember? Those are our great-grandchildren.

Husband: I know my great-grandchildren. Those are pictures of strangers.

Wife: No, they aren't strangers! See, that is Bill. There is Sara, and this one is Don. Repeat after me....

And, we're off and running!

Same people, but a little different approach...

Husband: Who are those strangers in the pictures on my dresser? Why are they there?

Wife: Kids sure grow up fast. I often think about our kids and their children. I like to see pictures of them.

Husband: I agree, but who are those strangers in the pictures on my dresser?

Wife: Those are Brad's grandchildren. They are our great-grandchildren! We only saw them when they were babies, so I can see how they look like strangers to you. They live in Colorado. I was thinking about the trip we took to Colorado. Boy, those mountains are something. I always felt so small in comparison to them. I liked the picnic we had in that national park.

Arguing almost always leads to anger and bad feelings for your loved one. With the goal of making the conversation pleasant and worthwhile for both of you, leave 'no' and 'don't you remember?' out of your vocabulary and focus on information your loved one has the highest potential of knowing.

SAVING FACE

I believe that very young children don't lie. Rather, they tell you what they wish were true. In many respects I see the same phenomenon occurring in folks with cognitive loss. Let's see how that might look.

Example One:

> Sister: I already took my bath earlier today.
> Brother: You never did. You know better than that. Your hair isn't clean.
> Sister: It must be the shampoo, because I took my bath and washed my hair.
> Brother: No, you are wrong.
> Sister: I am not!!

And, we're off and running!

Same people in a different conversation...

> Sister: I already took my bath earlier today.
> Brother: It's hard to stay warm when you're all wet!
> Sister: Yes, I don't like to take a bath when it's cold.
> Brother: I agree. It really gets cold when washing your hair.
> Sister: I know. That's why I didn't wash mine.
> Brother: I've got some great hair cleaner that doesn't need water. I'd like to show you.

Example Two:

Dad: I've got to talk to the workmen; they aren't doing a good job. I've been watching, and they are not doing right.

Daughter: You're retired. You don't have workmen working for you. Those people work for the nursing home.

Dad: No, they don't. They are supposed to work for me. Now, let me tell them what they are doing wrong.

Daughter: Hush! Don't raise your voice. You are embarrassing me!

And, we're off and running!

Same people in a different conversation...

Dad: I've got to talk to the workmen; they aren't doing a good job. I've been watching, and they aren't doing things right.

Daughter: I know you know how work should be done. Seeing workers not doing their best is frustrating to you.

Dad: You're right! Young people these days don't care.

Daughter: I was thinking about your old saying, "An honest day's work is all I ask of you."

Dad: Yep, I told everybody who worked for me that saying. And, I meant it too!

Or,

Dad: I've got to talk to the workmen; they aren't doing a good job. I've been watching and they aren't doing right.

Daughter: What do you think we could tell them?

Dad: First, tell them to stop standing around.

Daughter: Looks like you're going to have lots of good advice. Let me write it down as you talk.

Dad: We need to tell them to stop watching each other.

Daughter: Let me write that down... Stop watching each other. How many men did you supervise, Dad?

Dad: About 15.

Daughter: Was it hard supervising all those people?

And the topic, with luck, can be switched. If he truly were watching a group of people he thinks are his workers, the speaker could try to move away from the group as the conversation continued. This would reduce the stimulation for him regarding that issue.

A Dangerous Mindset: They Can Be Different If They Wanted To Be

No one wants to look out of control. This is also true for our loved ones with cognitive loss. They want to be present as much as possible. Comments they make are not to deceive or manipulate us, but are said to "save face."

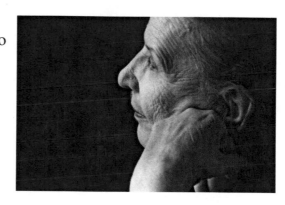

It is difficult, if not impossible, for many of us to admit we're wrong when we *don't* have memory loss. Everyone wants to look intelligent and in control. That is all that our loved ones are trying to do, too. They are trying to stay in the conversation as a strong and contributing person.

Thus, if the conversations are going to improve, change must occur on our side. We must believe that our loved ones are doing their best to communicate with us in light of their need to be seen as okay. We must accept them where they are, and not feel compelled to judge them as if they're doing something dishonest, such as lying or being manipulative.

They are telling us what they wish were true, what they think we want to hear, and/or what they actually believe is true. They are being as honest as they can be.

Adopting a positive attitude about their comments will take us far in talking successfully with them.

THEY CAN BE DIFFERENT

In order to avoid falling into the trap of thinking our loved ones can choose to be different, we must combine the two previous thoughts: they can't recall events in the recent past and we have to give them up as they used to be. When we truly understand these two concepts we can begin to enjoy our loved ones as the people they are today.

Example One:

Mom: I have trouble thinking clearly lately. I just can't remember things that just happened.

Son: Why can't you remember? You're just letting your brain go to mush. If you concentrate, you'll be able to remember better.

Mom: I'm trying my hardest. I guess I'm just no good to you anymore. I wish I were dead.

Son: Stop talking nonsense. I read an article that said working crossword puzzles can help memory so I bought you some.

Mom: I never did crossword puzzles in my life. I don't like them!

Son: I don't know what to do to help you. Everything I suggest you don't like.

And, we're off and running!

Same people, but in a little different conversation...

Mom: I have trouble thinking clearly lately. I just can't remember things that just happened.

Son: I bet that it is frustrating for you. Does writing things down help?

Mom: I don't remember to write things down.

Son: I like to hear you tell stories from the old days. Like the one you tell about the homemade wine. Do you have time to tell me that great story again?

Acknowledging your loved one's feelings of frustration tells them you are hearing what is being said. Dwelling on that frustration, however, can lead to an unpleasant feeling for both of you. When you see that "logical" solutions aren't working, attempt to move the conversation to a pleasant topic. Sometimes it helps to write down the pleasant stories. Later in the workbook is a section titled "Stories." This section allows you to record stories your loved one is fond of so you can recall them in times of frustration and use them as prompts for future conversations.

Example Two:

Niece arrives at her aunt's house and finds it very disorganized.

Niece: You aren't keeping your place tidy. Look at all of the magazines, papers, and old coffee cups all around.

Aunt: I was going to work on that today

Niece: You said that last time I was here. Your house used to be so neat. You always told me, "Cleanliness is next to Godliness." Now look at this place.

Aunt: I just don't have time. I get so tired. I like it like this anyway.

Niece: I don't believe you. You would never have lived with this mess in the old days.

Same people, but a little different conversation...

Niece: Do you have a copy of Tuesday's newspaper? I missed an article a friend of mine was telling me about.

Aunt: Well, as you can see the newspapers are all over the room. See if you can find it.

Niece: Do you have time to help me hunt? It's Tuesday's paper. March 20th.

Aunt: All right, but I can't work too long; I get tired.

Niece: I sure understand. Let's start and just pile up the ones that aren't the one we're looking for.

Asking assistance to accomplish a task often engages our loved ones. All people enjoy helping others. Using information we know about our loved ones' likes, we can ask for assistance in an area where they have, or at least had, an interest. We're working to capture their interest and attention on one topic.

How Should I Talk With My Loved One?

This all sounds very theoretical, but what would it sound like during a real conversation?

Let's look at an example of how to respond if your 85-year old mother said, "I've got to get going. I'm going shopping with my Mom."

What Not To Say

Attempting to bring her back into reality will only anger her or make her feel ignorant and not in control. You certainly do not want to say, "Your Mom is gone, and has been for 20 years." This can evoke all the feelings that were present when she first learned her Mom passed away.

You also wouldn't say, "You are 85, how old would your Mom be now?" We don't need a quiz at this point! This statement requires her to use skills she no longer has available and increases her agitation. You would also avoid saying, "Don't you remember?" The answer, if she could answer, would be, "No. I don't remember, and I feel inadequate, mad, confused, and scared."

Okay, So What Should I Say?

Live in your loved one's reality and try to match the same emotion he or she is showing. If your loved one is excited, be excited; if sad, be quiet. If your loved one is confused or worried, show empathy. If your loved one is happy, then join in the happiness. Your reaction to your loved one's actions or emotions demonstrates acceptance of these feelings and gives credence to them.

Look at your loved one's questions, comments, or emotions as an indication that an idea has just come to mind and your loved one wants to talk about it. Here are some key things to remember when talking with loved ones.

IT'S IMPORTANT TO ME BECAUSE IT'S IMPORTANT TO YOU

The key to effectively communicating with loved ones with cognitive loss is to make comments that show you are interested in what they are saying. Let them know you support their thinking.

A statement such as, "Tell me about your mom," lets them feel that their thoughts about their mom are okay, and that you are interested in the information.

YOU ARE RIGHT!

Next, acknowledge that what they are thinking has value and you are not judging the accuracy of what they said. Comments such as, "Your Mom was very important to you," or "The two of you loved to shop," demonstrates that you know their thoughts have value. They often feel comfort when they hear you make a statement showing you know them and the importance of what they are remembering.

TELL ME ABOUT...

Consider asking them a specific question about their parents or family using information you have from your history with them. There is a section in this workbook where you can enter these stories so they are at your fingertips.

Comments such as, "Tell me that story about when you had so many packages, they wouldn't fit in the car," or "Tell me about the time you bought that beautiful bowl."

Use information from stories from years ago. Think of stories or items that were talked about over the years, and then use these items as conversation starters.

I can hear you already saying, "Wait a minute. Earlier you said questions were not acceptable when talking with my loved one, isn't this just another question?" Well, yes, it would be if you asked, "Do you remember the time you bought that beautiful bowl?"

I know it sounds as if I'm splitting hairs, but how you ask a question is important. The goal is to prompt a memory, not test your loved one's memory.

Another approach might be to get involved in creating a shopping list. You could say, "Let's make a list of the stores you need to visit." You need to be ready with names of stores to "help" create this list.

Because you know your loved one's history, you hold the much needed information that can be the basis for your conversation about shopping.

In each example, your goal is to engage the loved one in pleasant conversation about a topic they have discussed long enough ago that the forgetfulness becomes your friend.

SHIFTING THE SUBJECT

If your loved one leaves you, thought-wise, follow the new subject. Stop discussing the issue that you were just discussing and bring up another topic that brings happiness to them. Telling a story such as, "I was thinking about the time we made taffy and I got it in my hair" might be just the ticket to changing subjects.

ACKNOWLEDGE FEELINGS

What if your loved one suddenly remembers information that had been forgotten, such as "I just remembered, my mom's dead."

It's important to respond with empathy to show that you understand that the memory is a sad one. These feelings could be just as fresh as they were when the death occurred.

A comment such as, "I'm sorry. I know you miss her," validates the feeling and shows you realize the importance of the matter.

LAUGHTER

It is almost impossible to be sad, mad, happy, and laughing all at the same time. If you can bring up a memory that evokes a good feeling, and hopefully laughter, you might be able to diffuse an anxious situation.

We must be careful never to laugh at our loved ones. Laughter aimed at them devalues and ridicules their thoughts.

An old family joke or story may be just the ticket to turn the anxious moment into a laugh-filled moment. Using your memories of times spent together with your loved one can provide humor from a real life situation that you know they found funny.

An example might be, "I was thinking about the time the dog ate the turkey just before Thanksgiving dinner." You need to know they think it's funny, not just a story you think is funny.

STARTING THE CONVERSATION

The techniques listed above work very well when loved ones start the conversation. They also work well in a conversation that you start. However, we need to talk about how to start a conversation.

To this point, the focus has been on responding to comments made by your loved one. The techniques explained so far are beneficial when the loved ones start the conversation, and can help you have a conversation. What about when you are responsible for starting and managing the conversation?

Selecting the topic, valuing your loved one's long term memory, and setting a pleasant, non-challenging atmosphere are the tools for success you will want to bring to the conversation.

See if this sounds familiar. You go to see your loved one, or call him or her on the phone. You truly want the visit to go well. However, you start with a common opening such as, "So, how are you today?" This often leads to a long response listing everything that isn't going well.

This occurred because the loved one was put in the position of managing the conversation. This is very challenging for anyone with cognitive loss. Remember, the desire to be normal is still present even if memory is not.

You need to prepare for your visit and consciously plan to open the conversation in a different manner. Remember, you want to manage the conversation in a calm, pleasant, and enjoyable manner.

YOUR HOMEWORK

How do you get ready for all of this talking? How do you manage conversations so the results are positive? How do you use your vast knowledge of your loved one positively?

Sorry to say, but it's just like everything else in life, it takes work! You need to do your homework and get ready to enjoy conversing with your loved one again. Following are the homework pages. These exercises are not difficult and will provide you with a valuable resource for future conversations.

Take time to complete each section. When you have completed this information, you will find you have created a wonderful tool chest of conversation starters. Whether you use these hints to respond to a loved one or to start a conversation, this personal workbook will be very important.

The use of old memories has been mentioned many times. You need to gather them and use them positively.

You might ask family and friends to help capture memories that your loved one will respond to. The more information you can gather, the better.

Make sure to capture old memories rather than very recent ones. You want to provide topics that have the best chance of triggering a pleasant memory. Let's get started remembering!

_____ LOVED TO SEE

Put your loved one's name, or the name you call him or her, in the blank. This will help you focus as you complete this page.

You are now creating a workbook of conversation items based on things your loved one enjoyed seeing. The more you have, the bigger your conversation tool kit.

You want to remember as many things that your loved one enjoyed seeing and enter these items below. Be specific. You should write, "white fluffy clouds on a bright summer day," rather than "clouds."

_____

_____

_____

_____

_____

_____

_____

_____

_____

_____

_____

_____

_____

LOVED TO SEE

LOVED TO SMELL

Put your loved one's name in the blank. This will help you focus as you complete this page.

You want to remember as many things that your loved one enjoyed smelling and enter these items below. Be specific; write, "clean laundry hanging on the line on a windy day" rather than, "clean clothes."

_____

_____

_____

_____

_____

_____

_____

_____

_____

_____

_____

_____

_____

_____

_____

LOVED TO SMELL

_____

_____

_____

_____

_____

_____

_____

_____

_____

_____

_____

_____

_____

_____

_____

_____

_____

LOVED TO TASTE

Put your loved one's name, or the name you call him or her, in the blank. This will help you focus as you complete this page.

You want to remember as many things that your loved one enjoyed tasting and enter these items below. Be specific; include descriptive words such as, "an angel food cake with almond flavoring" rather than, "cake."

_____

_____

_____

_____

_____

_____

_____

_____

_____

_____

_____

_____

_____

_____

_____

LOVED TO TASTE

LOVED TO TOUCH

Put your loved one's name, or the name you call him or her, in the blank. This will help you focus as you complete this page.

Remember, the more information you record, the bigger your conversation tool kit.

You want to remember as many things that your loved one enjoyed touching and enter these items below. Be specific; write "the soft, warm dirt when planting garden plants" rather than, "dirt."

_____

_____

_____

_____

_____

_____

_____

_____

_____

_____

_____

_____

_____

_____

LOVED TO TOUCH

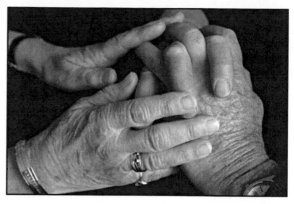

_____

_____

_____

_____

_____

_____

_____

_____

_____

_____

_____

_____

_____

_____

_____

_____

_____

_____

_____

_____

_____

LOVED TO HEAR

Put your loved one's name, or the name you call him or her, in the blank. This will help you focus as you complete this page.

You are now creating a workbook of conversation items based on things your loved one enjoyed hearing.

You want to remember as many things that your loved one enjoyed hearing and enter these items below. Be specific; write, "Ode To Joy from Beethoven's 9th Symphony" rather than, "music."

_____

_____

_____

_____

_____

_____

_____

_____

_____

_____

_____

_____

_____

_____

_____

_____

LOVED TO HEAR

STORIES THAT MAKE _____ HAPPY

Put your loved one's name, or the name you call him or her, in the blank. This will help you focus as you complete this page.

You are now creating a workbook of conversation items based on stories that made your loved one happy.

You want to remember as many stories that your loved one enjoyed and enter these stories below. You can just write a phrase to remind you of the story but be specific, such as "the time the dog ate the Thanksgiving turkey" rather than "Thanksgiving."

_____

_____

_____

_____

_____

_____

_____

_____

_____

_____

_____

_____

_____

_____

_____

_____

_____

STORIES THAT MAKE _____ HAPPY

_____

_____

_____

_____

_____

_____

_____

_____

_____

_____

_____

_____

_____

_____

_____

_____

_____

_____

_____

_____

STORIES THAT MAKE_____
UNHAPPY

Put your loved one's name, or the name you call him or her, in the blank. This will help you focus as you complete this page.

You are now creating a workbook of topics that you don't want to bring up as conversation starters. These are topics that do not bring your loved one happiness. Of course, if the loved one brings the stories up, you can use the techniques described earlier to talk with them. You can just write a phrase to remind you of the story, and again, be specific. Write, "loss of their home in the tornado," rather than "tornados."

_____

_____

_____

_____

_____

_____

_____

_____

_____

_____

_____

_____

_____

STORIES THAT MAKE_____
UNHAPPY

_____

_____

_____

_____

_____

_____

_____

_____

_____

_____

_____

_____

_____

_____

_____

_____

_____

_____

_____

_____

How To Use The Workbook

You are almost ready to start having pleasant conversations with your loved one who suffers from cognitive loss. Just one more step, and you will be ready.

Now that your homework is done, let's talk about how you can tie the concepts together with the information you gathered to help you have a successful conversation with your loved one.

As you are planning a visit with your loved one, take a few minutes to review the information in your workbook.

Select a few entries you want to use during your visit. Armed with this vital material, you are ready to have a good conversation.

When you start the conversation, the phrase, "*I was thinking*" works very well. It puts the focus on the topic without challenging your loved one to remember. It is difficult not to say, "Do you remember?" but with a little practice it will become much easier.

You can talk about the topic and determine if your loved one does remember. If so, and he or she can still speak, let your loved one share personal thoughts about the topic. If your loved one can't speak, you can still discuss the topic from your perspective and show your pleasure with the memory.

If your loved one doesn't seem to recognize the topic, you can change topics. If there is a topic that is consistently not useful, simply make a note in your workbook to leave that one alone for a while. It might become valuable at a later time.

If you start a conversation and your loved one goes to an unpleasant part of that topic, acknowledge the feelings and let the loved one remember a negative aspect of the story.

An example might be when you start talking to your dad about the family dog that used to bring your dad his slippers each night. That is a great story, and you know how much dad loved to tell it. However, that dog has passed away and your dad might remember that the dog is gone and talk about how much he misses the dog.

Allow him to talk about the dog and acknowledge the loss. Then, you could bring up another happy memory involving the dog.

Probably the most important aspect of the I Was Thinking approach is that it allows people with cognitive loss to join conversations at their comfort level. If they want to discuss a topic, then let them share. If they include information that you don't recall, let it go.

The future of the world will not be made or broken based on their understanding of the topic. However, the future of our relationships with our loved ones often depends on our reactions to their attempts to become involved in conversations.

This is really the culmination of giving them up to find them where they are. Validating their memory of the topic provides them with support and comfort in being successful in talking with you.

I Was Thinking Examples

When you arrive to visit with your loved one, make sure you have a smile on your face and have no expectations that your loved one can and/or will manage the conversation.

After the initial kisses and hugs, or whatever salutation is typical for you and your loved one, you're ready to begin the conversation.

Of course, you will want to remember and use topics that you have written in this workbook. The following are examples of how simple it is to use the information you have gathered as you strive for pleasant conversations with your loved one.

USING WHAT THEY LOVED TO SEE:

"I was thinking about beautiful red roses with dew on them. I know you loved to see them, and the dewdrops just glistened, as I recall. You had rose bushes with clusters and clusters of roses. It must have taken a lot of work, but they looked perfect to me. I bet it was hard to keep them trimmed and looking so good. I always wondered what your secret was."

Or,

"I was thinking about the family picture we had taken in your front yard. There must have been over 50 people in that one picture! I know you loved that picture, and would like to see it again. I think it's in the photo album over there." (Gesture to the photo album you created with their favorite pictures and gave to them at a previous visit.) "That was such a fun day for me. I sometimes try to name everyone in the picture."

These examples demonstrate that once you have presented the topic, make a comment your loved one could respond to if they wish. Don't rush them or push them for their involvement. Sometimes, simply sitting quietly and smiling will prompt them to start to speak. If not, you can continue with other aspects of the story in a reminiscent mode.

USING WHAT THEY LOVED TO SMELL:

"I was thinking about the wonderful smell of that delicious bread you used to make. You always told me how you loved that smell, and actually used it to keep me in the house after school! I would come home and have to decide between running outside with my friends, or staying in the house with you and having just one slice of that warm bread with lots of butter. I wonder if I could learn to make that bread like you did. I think I'd need your secret!"

Or,

"I was thinking about that perfume you loved. It came in that neat blue bottle and sometimes you'd let me use it! You told me that you always felt so beautiful when you had that perfume on. I bet you wore it for special occasions."

USING WHAT THEY LOVED TO TASTE:

"I was thinking about how you and I would have Limburger and onion on rye bread sandwiches! You always told me we could have them, but then we couldn't talk to anyone until that smell went away! You used to put pepper on your sandwich. What do you think makes that Limburger smell so bad?"

Or,

"I was thinking about those smelt you loved so. You would get a keg of those fish and then pass them out to our family very carefully to make them last longer. I always loved those kegs after they were empty. I wonder who caught those fish and how they got them into those kegs?"

USING WHAT THEY LOVED TO TOUCH:

"I was thinking about how you loved new puppies and like touching their soft bellies! How can they be that soft? And their coats were so smooth. You loved to cuddle the puppies and pet them. I wonder why their coats used to change from so soft to a little more wiry when they grew up?"

Or,

"I was thinking about how you used to tell me how good it felt to hug your grandchildren. You said they were so vulnerable and too strong at the same time. I always thought that was funny. How could they be both at the same time? You said the greatest feeling was when they hugged you so hard you had to say "Uncle," and then they would laugh and laugh. How many times did you have to say "Uncle" before they'd let go? Can I have a hug right now?"

USING WHAT THEY LOVED TO HEAR:

"I was thinking about that song you loved, The Prisoner's Song. You used to play it for me on the piano and make that great run of music with the back of your fingers. How did you do that without hurting your fingers?"

Or,

"I was thinking about how you loved the sound of a smoothly running car engine. You always told me you could tell if you had fixed it properly because it was "purring like a kitten." Other car mechanics had to step back when you walked down the street. Where did you learn how to fix cars?"

USING THE STORIES THAT THEY LOVED:

"I was thinking about the time you told me about flying a plane to Mom's house to date her. You said you would land the small plane in her dad's field, and she was the envy of all of the neighbor girls. The picture of you and that plane is right here in this album. How far could you fly it before you needed to refuel?"

Or,

"I was thinking about the trip to California your family took when you were a child. You said you were young, but you remember that there wasn't any air conditioning in cars in those days and it was hot! The car overheated, and the car almost didn't make it up a twisting mountain road! I wonder if you ate in restaurants or had picnics during the trip?"

As you look at the examples, you will find that many of them touch on more than one area. That is logical since people are very complex and all aspects of life really do dovetail in many cases. This is really a plus and will help you move from one topic to another more easily.

LENGTH OF A VISIT

Don't feel as if you need to talk for a long time. Several short visits are often more appreciated and valued than a long visit. Perhaps you've been reluctant to visit in the past because you didn't know what to say, or were worried that the visit would turn sour with negative emotions.

If you've done your homework, you now have many topics to talk about which will serve you for many visits. Take advantage of the work you have done and consider having several short visits rather than a few long and possibly unpleasant visits.

SAYING GOODBYE

One last thought. Think about how you leave your loved one with cognitive loss. Normally, when you are ready to leave after visiting with friends, you simply say, "Goodbye." However, since your loved one is often taking the clue for his or her "proper" action from others, this word might prompt them to think they need to leave also. This is particularly true if your loved one lives in a place that is not their home, such as a long-term care facility.

If your loved one's thinking prompts them to leave with you, the last few minutes you spend with them can be uncomfortable.

There is no fool-proof way to leave that will work 100 percent of the time. Here are a few possible approaches.

Try stating what you are going to do.
• I've got to do the wash.
• I'm going to the gym.
• I'm late to pick up the dog.

Perhaps you will have good results by diverting attention from your leaving with statements such as:
• I see people are getting ready for dinner. I'll get going.
• I noticed there is a singing group entertaining down the hall. I'll help you find a good seat before I head out for the night.

If you know that your leaving upsets your loved one, consider not saying anything about it. Perhaps you can simply leave the area with one of these statements:
• I've got to go to the bathroom.
• I need to check on the kids.
• I'm going to get a drink.

You might wonder if this should be considered "lying" to them. Remember, their inability to process information correctly makes their understanding of your leaving without them very difficult. What you're doing with these types of statements is providing them a logical reason for why you are walking away from them without stirring up any anxiety at the prospect of you leaving them.

Maybe the easiest parting line might be, "I love you. Talk soon."

And, with all the information you have gathered and written down, you will have lots to talk about the next time you visit.

YOU NEED THE EQUIPMENT
AT YOUR FINGERTIPS

As you read the examples, perhaps you started thinking about the value of having the right items available to help you during the conversation. You are absolutely correct. Items that have meaning to your loved one need to be accessible so you can utilize them and share the items with your loved one.

Significant things such as picture albums, old scrapbooks, books that relate to their favorite things such as books on fishing, trains, horses, cooking, knitting, etc., need to be available. You also want to make sure that old letters, jewelry, religious items, favorite clothing, pillows, and plants are also available. The list will be almost endless.

Think of these items as "props" to work with as you bring up various topics. Think in terms of the things that are significant to you in your home. Look around, and you will notice you have the items you love most close to you. The same is true for your loved one. Unfortunately, they often forget where those items are located. You can bring pleasure to them by talking about their items while you are actually holding, touching, or looking at them.

Meeting
The Challenge

It's so easy for me to write what to do. Yet, I personally know how challenging it is talking with a loved one with cognitive loss. I don't have all of the answers. No one does. Your goal is to increase the number of pleasant, calm conversations, and reduce the number of confrontations and frustrations caused by unsuccessful conversations.

Please know that not every conversation will be stellar. Accept that you are human and will say things that you will later wish had gone unsaid. Forgive yourself, and start over the next day.

Reward yourself for each and every successful conversation. Remember the happiness on your loved one's face or the twinkle in his or her eyes as you both talked about a favorite memory. Become conscious of the good you are doing by finding new ways to converse with your loved one. Please do not forget to find time for yourself. The sadness and frustration of seeing your loved one dealing with cognitive loss does not go away simply because the conversations are good. You have feelings that need to be addressed as well.

Find a friend, an organization, or a church support group that understands and will allow you to talk about you. The trail you are blazing is very important to both you and your loved one. Take it one step at a time. Remember, there will be stones along the way; take comfort that you aren't walking that trail alone.

———————■———————

20 KEY POINTS TO SUCCESSFUL CONVERSATIONS

1. Giving up expectations allows you to find the loved one that is still there. (Pg. 9)
2. Don't assume that your loved one is being manipulative or deceptive. (Pg. 13 & 23)
3. "NO" is a negative message that devalues their thoughts and wishes. (Pg. 13)
4. They have trouble living in your reality, but you CAN live in theirs. (Pg. 14)
5. Refrain from challenging your loved one with "Don't You Remember?" (Pg. 17)
6. Help you loved one to save face. (Pg. 20)
7. They are who they are, they do not have the ability to be different. (Pg. 23 & 24)
8. If something is important to them, let them know it's important to you. (Pg. 28)
9. Acknowledge that what they are thinking has value. (Pg.28)
10. "Tell me about......" can elicit the good memory out of a sad one.(Pg.28)
11. Always acknowledge your loved ones feelings. (Pg.29)
12. Help them laugh at things they think are funny. (Pg. 29)
13. Take time to write down things that are important to your loved one. (Pgs 32-45)
14. Before you visit review your workbook and select a few topics. (Pg. 46)

continued...

20 KEY POINTS TO SUCCESSFUL CONVERSATIONS, CONT.

15. Start conversations with the phrase "I was thinking about..." (Pg. 47)
16. Five senses provide personal information that turn into conversations. (Pg. 47-50)
17. Short visits with contented conversation win over long "dutiful" visits. (Pg. 51)
18. Leaving might cause confusion for your loved one. (Pg.52)
19. Meaningful personal belongings provide conversation material. (Pg.53)
20. Reward yourself for each successful conversation and take care of you! (Pg. 54)

———————— ■ ————————

ABOUT THE AUTHOR

A sought after speaker and consultant, Diana has cared for older adults and taught others to do the same for more than 30 years. However, her best insight into the subject came while caring for her mother who suffered from cognitive loss.

Diana shares simple ideas to help you approach conversations differently by using stories and memories you grew up with as conversation starters. She also provides pages for you to record these story ideas so you can create a "conversation toolkit."

Diana says it is important to identify happy stories and memories from your loved one's past and use them to have calm, enjoyable conversations. "Probably one of the most difficult approaches to having good conversations is to let go of our expectations of our loved ones," states Diana. "The most challenging yet most rewarding approach to talking with loved ones with cognitive loss is to learn to live in their reality, not ours."